P9-CAO-451

Translation – Christine Schilling
Adaptation – Mallory Reaves
Lettering – Monalisa J. de Asis
Production Assistant – Suzy Wells
Editorial Assistant –Mallory Reaves
Production Manager – James Dashiell
Editor – Brynne Chandler

A Go! Comi manga

Published by Go! Media Entertainment, LLC

Black Sun Silver Moon Volume 7
© 2008 TOMO MAEDA
All rights reserved.
First published in Japan in 2008 by SHINSHOKAN Co., Ltd. Tokyo
English Version published by Go! Media Entertainment, LLC under license
from SHINSHOKAN Co., Ltd.

Visit us online at www.gocomi.com
e-mail: info@gocomi.com

ISBN 978-1-60510-027-2

First printed in November 2008

1 2 3 4 5 6 7 8 9

Manufactured in the United States of America

黒の太陽 銀の月

7

前田とも
TOMO MAEDA

CONTENTS

A Place Where the Birds Don't Fly

鳥も通わぬ場所

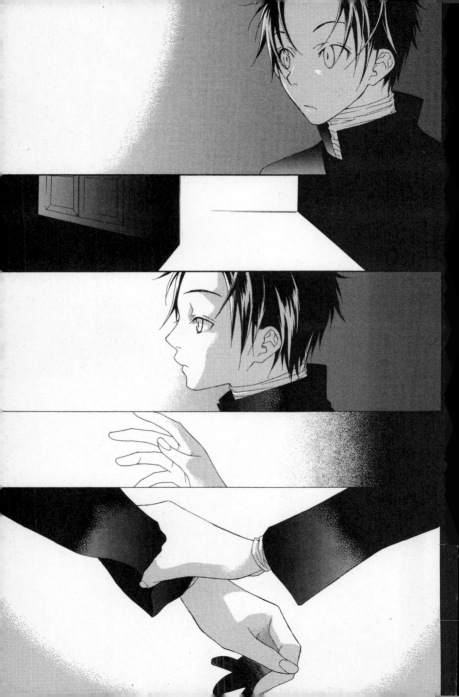

SEN...

DID I...

...MAKE IT IN TIME?

SENSEI...

THAT DOOR...

WELL, WELL, WELL.

HE'LL BE FINE. I STOPPED HIM.

HE MUST HAVE REALIZED.

SOMEONE DOESN'T KNOW WHEN TO GIVE UP.

YES, THAT'S RIGHT.

YOU'RE LUCKY YOU DIDN'T HAVE TO USE FORCE.

POOR THING, HAVING TO LOOK DEATH IN THE FACE SO OFTEN.

HE'LL END UP HERE EVENTUALLY, EITHER WAY.

IT'S A PITY.

DON'T YOU THINK?

OH, IT IS...

YOU'RE GETTING AHEAD OF YOURSELVES. HE HASN'T DIED YET.

AND I WON'T LET HIM!

I'M... I'M HERE BECAUSE OF YOU.

OH, REALLY?

AND HOW ARE YOU GOING TO STOP IT?

LET ME GO. PLEASE! THERE'S STILL SO MUCH I HAVE TO DO—

YOU'RE HELPLESS HERE. WHAT CAN YOU DO?

WE CAN'T.

YOU CAN'T LEAVE. NO ONE CAN.

WE'RE JUST LIKE YOU, SWALLOWED UP BY THE LITTLE DEMONS. WE'RE ALL VICTIMS.

WE'RE IN THE BELLY OF THE BEAST. LITERALLY.

BET YOU'VE NEVER SEEN SUCH A LARGE STOMACH, HUH?

....

YOU CAN STILL SEE WHAT GOES ON OUTSIDE, RIGHT?

UNLESS WE'RE CALLED OUT, WE CAN ONLY LINGER IN DARKNESS.

VERY FUNNY.

WE CAN IMAGINE WHAT'S GOING ON OUT THERE.

WHY ARE YOU LETTING THIS CONTINUE!?

IF YOU'RE ALL VICTIMS, YOU'VE SEEN THE DESTRUCTION THIS THING CAUSES! YOU'VE SEEN HOW MANY PEOPLE HAVE DIED!

LAZ...?

WHA—

IT'S NO USE GETTING ANGRY.

WE'VE SEEN IT ENOUGH TO KNOW.

WE HAVE NO CONSCIENCE OR SYMPATHY.

THE DEMONS ALLOW US ONLY HATRED, LOATHING, SUFFERING AND SADNESS. THERE'S NO USE GETTING ANGRY.

FRAGMENTS OF MEMORIES SWALLOWED BY THE DEMONS.

TO BE MORE SPECIFIC, WE ARE MERELY PIECES OF SOULS.

BUT I SUPPOSE YOU'RE DIFFERENT

YOUR HEART WAS ALREADY TAKEN FROM YOU.

THAT IS...

...YOUR OTHER HALF.

IF YOU UNDERSTAND, YOU WON'T TRY TO FIGHT IT.

NOTHING YOU DO WILL HELP.

THAT IS WHAT'S TAKING YOUR FORM OUTSIDE.

THERE MUST BE A WAY TO GET BACK.

!

FINE... SO IT'S HOPELESS, IS IT?

I GOT HERE SOMEHOW. THERE MUST BE A WAY TO GET OUT.

LAZ?

WHAT AM I...

I SAW TAKI HERE. IF IT REALLY WAS HIM, THERE MUST BE...

NO...

SHOVE

FSS!!

STOP!!

GYAAH!!

AH!

Oh, I can move again.

!?

HUH!?

HACK ...GAH!!

SPLISH

WHA...?

SH... SHIKIMI!?

OH, GOOD.

I WAS HOPING THAT WOULD WORK.

......

I KNEW YOU COULDN'T RESIST THE HUNGER.

GLUTTONY IS A SIN, YOU KNOW.

JUST A SIP WOULD HAVE SUFFICED.

YANK

SHIKI-

!?

!

COUGH

THIS IS...

WHAT DID YOU DO TO HER...!?

ALL THAT BLOOD CAN'T BE FROM ME.

WHAT HAPPENED?

BUT...! HE'S THROWING UP...

HE JUST TOOK A BITE OUT OF YOU, REMEMBER?

WHAT'RE YOU DOING? I'M TRYING TO SAVE YOU!

DON'T WORRY, HE'LL BE FINE.

He's immortal, as you may recall.

IT WON'T DO MUCH MORE THAN SLOW HIM DOWN.

HE MAY HAVE A TOUCH OF INDIGESTION, THOUGH.

GO ON, RUN AWAY!

FREEZE

HOLY WATER...!

||||

IT'S JUST A LITTLE INJECTION.

WHA... WH-WH- WHAT'RE YOU GONNA DO!?

DON'T WORRY.

NOW, THEN.

SALT WATER. IT'S HARMLESS.

SALT WATER!?

IT'S CALLED A SALINE SOLUTION.

IT'S THE SAME CONSISTENCY AS YOUR BLOOD.

YUP.

IT'S JUST A PRECAUTION.

COME HERE.

Oh. !

YOU WON'T EVEN REMEMBER IT'S THERE.

...IT WAS THE BEST WAY TO TRAP YOU WITHOUT HARMING HER.

IT'LL BE OUT OF HER SYSTEM IN ABOUT A MONTH. BUT MEANWHILE...

SALT WATER AND HOLY WATER ARE ABOUT THE SAME THING, AFTER ALL.

OF COURSE, THAT'S A SECRET TO DEMON VANQUISHERS.

Heh heh heh...

SHRUG

WHATEVER DO YOU MEAN?

WHAT ARE YOU...

DON'T PLAY DUMB WITH ME.

YOU WERE SUPPOSED TO BE ONE OF US.

WHY ARE YOU SIDING WITH THE HUMANS!?

...TRYING TO DO?

THAT'S ODD. DID YOU FORGET?

ARE YOU REALLY SHIKIMI?

OR DO YOU NOT KNOW?

YOU TOLD ME TO PROTECT THE CHILDREN.

THREE YEARS AGO...

...I PROMISED TO GRANT YOU A WISH IF YOU WON OUR BET.

!

YOU...

I'LL DO ANY ONE THING YOU ASK.

WANNA MAKE...

...A BET?

AND YOU DID.

SO...

...I KEPT MY PROMISE.

SO?

WHAT'LL IT BE? WHAT DO YOU WANT?

YOU MISER.

I'M NOT BEING A MISER.

WANNA BE HUMAN AGAIN?

YES. BUT THAT'S NOT SOMETHING YOU CAN GIVE ME.

I'M JUST BEING PRACTICAL.

I can't believe you just said that...

You're no help!!

I SAID I'D DO ANY ONE THING. THAT MEANS ONE PERSON, SO CHOOSE.

I KNOW. I JUST WANTED TO SAY IT.

IF THINGS TAKE A TURN FOR THE WORSE...I WANT YOU TO PROTECT TAKI AND LAZ FROM ME.

NOW WHO'S BEING A MISER!?

PLEASE.

WHAT'S GOING ON WITH HIM?

SHI—

·····

BLOCK

BUT... BUT I—

LISTEN.

IF YOU WANT TO DIE, I'LL LET YOU.

WHAT'RE YOU—

QUIT STALLING. GO HIDE SOME-WHERE.

BUT IF NOT, THINK ABOUT WHAT YOU'RE DOING.

ATTACKING HIM HEAD ON WILL GET YOU NOWHERE. RUN AND HIDE FOR NOW, AND FIND AN OPENING LATER.

WAIT....!

DON'T THINK I'LL PROTECT YOU FOREVER.

WHAT...

...ABOUT TAKI?

I SAID, WAIT!!

GRAB

WHA-!?

SMOOSH

HE'LL BE HERE SOON.

ALIVE...

EITHER WAY, DON'T INTERRUPT.

...OR DEAD.

IT'S BEEN SO LONG, I JUST WANT TO...

I HAVE A LITTLE SOMETHING...

...TO ASK THEM.

...SAY HELLO.

SOMETHING TO ASK THEM?

That was a greeting, not a question.

BLOCK

SWISH

BASH

RETREAT

...WHAT IS IT?

...ARE YOU?

WHAT...

?

OH, YES.

NOW I REMEMBER. WE'VE SEEN YOU BEFORE.

YOU DON'T EVEN ASK *WHO* I AM? HOW RUDE.

YOU SHOULDN'T TALK THAT WAY TO STRANGERS!

YES...I'VE SEEN IT COUNTLESS TIMES...

IT'S LIKE YOU'RE CHASING US. FOR WHAT PURPOSE?

I REMEMBER YOUR FACE.

WHAT'S THE MATTER? IT TAKES THAT MUCH CONCENTRATION TO REMEMBER SOMETHING?

MUST BE TOUGH, CRAMMING SO MANY SOULS INTO ONE BEING.

BUT I DON'T BLAME YOU...

I CAN'T EXPECT YOU TO REMEMBER EVERYONE YOU'VE KILLED.

...HUH?

DOES... DOES THAT MEAN HE...?

I SEE.

RUSTLE

OH, PLEASE.

I'M NOT INTERESTED IN THAT.

SO THIS IS REVENGE, THEN?

THAT'S WHY YOU'VE PURSUED US THIS FAR?

RUSTLE RUSTLE

RUSTLE

WE'RE THE SAME NOW, YOU AND I.

TMP TMP TMP TMP

REVENGE?

Agi...

!

EVERYONE DIES, EVENTUALLY.

SURE, I THINK MY TIME CAME A LITTLE EARLY, BUT THAT'S OKAY.

IT DOESN'T BOTHER ME, ANYMORE.

ALTHOUGH I WOULD HATE TO THINK...

IT'D BE A LITTLE SILLY...

...TO HOLD GRUDGES LIKE THAT FOR THIS LONG.

...BE TRAPPED IN THERE WITH THEM.

...THAT SHE MIGHT...

RIGHT INSIDE...

...THERE.

THEN...

...WHY HAVE YOU COME?

YOU CARE LITTLE FOR SELF-RIGHTEOUS REVENGE.

YOU ARE NOT BOTHERED BY...

...THE PEOPLE WE HAVE KILLED TO FEED.

YOU NEVER THOUGHT TWICE ABOUT STRIKING DOWN ENEMIES, OR FRIENDS.

...ALLOWING YOUR HUMAN EMOTIONS REIGN ONLY WHEN YOU CHOOSE.

YOU MOVE AS YOU WISH...

IS THERE SOME DEEP ATTACHMENT THAT KEEPS YOU COMING BACK?

FOR EXAMPLE...

SO WHY DO YOU CARE ABOUT US SO MUCH?

...SOME-ONE...

...YOU CARED ABOUT?

SOMEONE WITH HAIR LIKE SPUN GOLD...

WHO...

WHO IS THAT!?

MORE IMPORTANTLY...WHAT'S GOING ON HERE!?

...AND EYES YOU COULD NEVER FORGET?

AAAH... IT'S SO BRIGHT OUT HERE.

I'D FORGOTTEN HOW DAZZLING THE SUN CAN BE.

IT'S SO BRIGHT I CAN BARELY KEEP MY EYES OPEN.

MY DEAR...

...GREY.

I KNOW YOU'RE RIGHT THERE, BUT...

...MY EYES AREN'T USED TO THE LIGHT. WON'T YOU COME TO ME?

AAAH...

THERE YOU ARE.

STAB

TSK!

SLIP

GRAB

YOU'RE SO CRUEL.

YOU WERE GOING TO LEAVE ME AGAIN, WEREN'T YOU?

EITHER HE'LL DROP HIS GUARD, OR I'LL FORCE IT.

EVERYTHING HAS A WEAKNESS.

DON'T FORGET THAT.

FOR EXAMPLE...

I'LL MAKE HIM LET HIS GUARD DOWN.

EVEN IF I HAVE TO...

I CAN DISTRACT HIM.

IF OUR POSITIONS ARE REVERSED, I WON'T HOLD BACK. YOU SHOULDN'T, EITHER.

...LET HIM HURT ME.

BUT, CHANCES ARE...

...IT'LL BE UP TO YOU, AS A NIGHTLING, TO DELIVER THE FINAL BLOW.

FLASH

PAUSE

TAKI...

BASH

DASH

!!

TCH!

HEY!

ARE YOU OKAY!? HANG IN THERE...

!

AH...

!

SEN...

......!

KICK

GREY—

OH.

UH...

He sure is lively for his condition.

UUUUGH, I DON'T *BELIEVE* YOU!!

DIDN'T YOU LISTEN TO A THING I SAID? I THOUGHT WE HAD AN AGREEMENT!

SORRY...?

WH... WHAT DO YOU THINK YOU'RE DOING!?

GRAB

REALLY, YOU'RE RIGHT. IT WAS MY FAULT.

I DIDN'T EXPECT TO SEE HIM LIKE THAT—

FORGET IT,

THAT'S MY LINE, YOU *IDIOT!!*

IF SHIKIMI MAKES IT TO THE NEXT VILLAGE, YOU KNOW WHAT WILL HAPPEN.

DO YOU WANT TO BE RESPONSIBLE FOR THAT!?

JUST GO AFTER HIM!

BUT I WON'T HAVE THEM TORMENTING ANY MORE SOULS!

I DON'T CARE IF HE KILLS THE WHOLE VILLAGE.

TO BE HONEST, I DON'T CARE.

ACTUALLY, IT DOESN'T MATTER. ALL YOU NEED TO KNOW IS THAT THIS IS YOUR DUTY.

AND IF YOU CAN'T DO IT, GET OUT OF MY WAY!

DO YOU UNDERSTAND WHAT ETERNAL DARKNESS MEANS?

THAT'S WHAT HAPPENS WHEN THE DEMONS TRAP SOULS.

FINE... I'M SORRY.

I'LL DO IT.

WAAAH!!

TAKIIII!!!

GLOMP

Group hug!

THUD

WHAT HAPPENED TO Y—

!!!?

I said hurry!!

LAZ?

YOUR HAIR...

BUT...WHO WAS THAT WOMAN...?

!

SLIP

TAKI!

HEY!

Uh...

YEAH... I'M HERE.

ARE YOU OKAY!? SHOULD YOU BE WALKING!?

SNIFFLE

THANK GOD YOU'RE ALIVE!!

I THOUGHT YOU WERE A GONER! THANK GOODNESS!!

LICK LICK

PAT

EVERY-THING WILL BE OKAY.

LEAVE IT TO ME.

WHAT ABOUT YOU? YOU'VE BEEN THROUGH A LOT.

You're a mess...

YEAH, I'M FINE NOW.

Take his place, he says...

YOU OWE HIM FOR SAVING YOUR LIFE. THANKS!

Take my place, for once.

WAIT... BUT...I... TAKI!?

...WHAT!?

MEAN-WHILE, TAKE CARE OF HIM, WOULD YOU?

And Agi, too.

TOSS

Oh, no!

LICK LICK

LICK

BYE!

Ah!

DON'T WORRY... YOU CAN LEAVE ME.

OR WOULD YOU RATHER...

I'LL HEAL... WITH TIME.

...PLAY THE PART OF A DEMON VANQUISH-ER...

IF YOU'RE GONNA DO IT...NOW'S YOUR CHANCE.

...AND FINISH ME OFF?

JUST DO IT–!

GO AHEAD.

YANK

...HUH?

YOU SHOULDN'T BOTHER. I'M PRETTY HEAVY.

STRAIN

| | | | |

QUIT COMPLAINING, AND SAVE YOUR ENERGY!

HEFT

MMPH!

YOU SAVED ME BEFORE, SO NOW WE'LL BE EVEN.

I...I CAN'T JUST LEAVE. TAKI PUT ME IN CHARGE OF YOU!

BESIDES...

THERE'S NO SNOW THERE...

...SO IT SHOULD BE A LITTLE WARMER.

I'LL TAKE YOU OVER TO THAT TREE.

...THANKS.

I...

I'LL BE FINE. I'LL BE FINE. I'LL BE FINE!!

I REALLY WISH SHE'D LEFT ME WHERE I WAS.
This holy water reeks.

IF ONLY..

Heh...

...THERE WASN'T STILL HOLY WATER IN YOUR VEINS...

WHSPR

CHILL

EITHER WAY...

I CAN'T BELIEVE THEY PULLED THAT...

SHE ALWAYS WAS MANIPULATIVE.

HOW LIKE HER TO TREAT HER HUSBAND SO.

AFTER ALL, I ALWAYS SAID SHE WAS COLD AS ICE.

AND SHE WAS... BUT...

BUT...

...SHE'S WITHIN SHIKIMI.

BUT NOW I KNOW...

I CAN'T DO...

...ANYTHING ANYMORE.

HOW WRETCHED.

BUT I SUPPOSE... I CAN'T BLAME HIM.

SUCH A SNEAKY MAN.

JUST PRETENDING SHOCK AT SEEING ME AGAIN...

BUT...

OF COURSE HE'D CHANGE WITH THE SEASONS.

HOW MUCH TIME HAS PASSED IN THE OUTSIDE WORLD, I WONDER...

...AND THAT HE'D BEEN WAITING FOR ME ALL THIS TIME.

IT TRICKED ME INTO THINKING HIS HEART HADN'T CHANGED, EITHER...

THE BRUSH OF TIME HASN'T TOUCHED HIM AT ALL.

...HE STILL LOOKS LIKE HE DID BACK THEN.

HOW CRUEL...

...OF HER.

WHY...?

IF YOU ARE ALL MERELY FRAGMENTS OF MEMORIES...

IF THERE'S NO CONSCIENCE OR SYMPATHY LEFT...WHAT DO I SENSE IN YOUR HEART RIGHT NOW?

IT WASN'T TRUE, WAS IT? YOU CAN FEEL THE PASSING OF YEARS. YOU CAN FEEL PAIN.

YOU'RE NOT LOST SPIRITS, YOU STILL KNOW WHO YOU ARE! YOU KNOW YOU'RE DEAD! DO YOU REALLY WANT TO STAY THIS WAY!?

YOUR FEELINGS CONTRADICT WHAT YOU TOLD ME BEFORE.

DON'T TRY TO TELL ME YOU FELT NOTHING AT SEEING HIM AGAIN.

BUT SHOULDN'T YOU BE WORRYING ABOUT YOURSELF?

YOU'RE RIGHT ON THE MARK, SENSEI.

YOU'RE VERY PASSIONATE.

HUH...?

TAKE A LOOK.

SEE?

!

LET ME TELL YOU HOW THINGS WORK HERE.

SOMETIMES... WE FEEL. WE HATE, AND ACHE, AND WE REBEL.

YOU'RE RIGHT.

WE'RE NOT JUST GHOSTS WHO DON'T KNOW WE'VE DIED.

EVEN THIS HALF-LIFE IS BETTER THAN NOTHING AT ALL.

BUT IT'S ONLY FOR A MOMEN...

ALL OF US HAVE CHOSEN LIFE OVER EMOTION.

OTHERWISE, WE'D VANISH COMPLETELY. THE DEMONS WOULD SEE TO IT.

IT'S STRANGE, ISN'T IT?

AFTER ALL, IT'S NOT MUCH OF A LIFE. WE'RE TRAPPED HERE.

SO WHAT WILL IT BE?

WILL YOU FIGHT, KNOWING THAT YOU COULD BE EXTINGUISHED FOREVER?

BUT...

IS SHE TELLING ME TO GIVE IN?

IS SHE REALLY TELLING ME TO CLOSE MY HEART, FORGET EVERYTHING, AND LIVE THIS LIFE OF NOTHINGNESS?

...IF I DON'T, I'LL HAVE NOTHING. NOT EVEN MEMORIES.

ISN'T THAT NO BETTER THAN DYING?

THERE'S NO NEED TO CHARGE FATE HEAD-ON.

YES.

THAT'S THE WAY TO DO IT.

JUST PRETEND YOU'RE A LITTLE ROCK, SILENT AND IMPASSIVE.

IT'S NOT HARD...

YES.

MAYBE YOU'RE RIGHT.

I DON'T BELIEVE YOU.

IT'D BE EASIER TO JUST THROW AWAY ALL HOPE.

AFTER I WAS REALLY TRYING TO HELP...

BUT I CAN'T.

AND BEING ALIVE...

AFTER ALL, I'M STILL ALIVE.

BEING ALIVE MEANS...

CAN I...

...REALLY DO IT?

...AND...

I'LL TRACK HIM DOWN...

CORNER HIM...

DO I WANT TO KILL HIM?

...CAN I KILL HIM?

NO...

I
DON'T.

BUT...

BUT...

I'VE NEVER SEEN THIS PLACE.

WHAT IS THIS PLACE?

TAKI, DO YOU KNOW...

THERE'S NO SNOW...

...AND I SMELL FLOWERS.

COULD IT BE...

BUT, I THINK...

I'VE NEVER BEEN HERE BEFORE.

IT'S LITTLE MORE THAN A GRAVEYARD NOW, BUT...

...AND WHAT HAPPENED HERE?

...WHERE WE ARE...

...THIS IS MY VILLAGE.

I DON'T KNOW...

...IF IT'S WHAT I WANT ANYMORE.

AND I'M NOT AFRAID.

I NEED IT. LIKE I NEED THE AIR TO BREATHE.

BUT...

YOU KNOW, TAKI...

...IF I GO ANY FARTHER, I COULD LOSE ALL CHANCE OF LIFE AGAIN.

SO...

...LET US HAVE OUR MATCH...

...AND ALLOW FATE TO DECIDE THE VICTOR.

REACH

CLANG

SMACK

Urgh!

BLOCK

FSS!

GRAB

COUGH

NNGH...

BASH

SWIPE

......

!!

ALMOST...

...THERE!

WAH!!

!

SLIP

SLICE

PLOP

...AH.

‥‥‥‥‥

WHAT'S THE MATTER?

......

I'M GLAD WE'RE ABLE TO PLAY, BUT...

...AT THIS RATE, I'LL SIMPLY DIE OF BOREDOM.

OR IS THAT REALLY ALL YOU'VE GOT?

TAKI?

AND EVEN THOUGH I KNOW IT'S JUST SENSEI'S VOICE AND SENSEI'S FACE...

...DAMMIT.

EVEN THOUGH I KNOW I HAVE TO WIN...

...I JUST CAN'T FIGHT HIM FULL-ON.

BUT STILL...

HE'S RIGHT. I'M NOT REALLY TRYING.

MY SHOULDER IS KILLING ME...

EVEN IF I DID TRY MY BEST...

MY SHOULDER!

THUD

...IT PROBABLY WOULDN'T DO ANY GOOD.

GRIP

......!!!

OH, THAT'S RIGHT.

YOU'RE INJURED. I'M SORRY.

GYAAH!!

WHAT HAPPENED TO THAT FIRE YOU USED AGAINST GREY?

...THIS CANNOT POSSIBLY BE THE TRUE STRENGTH OF A NIGHTLING.

REGARDLESS...

OH, THAT'S RIGHT. YOU DON'T REMEMBER.

WHAT?

!

YOU CAN'T EVEN USE THE GIFTS YOU WERE BORN WITH.

AS A THE NATURAL ENEMY OF THE RESUR-RECTED...

...I CAN'T BELIEVE THIS IS ALL YOU'VE GOT WHEN YOUR LIFE IS AT STAKE.

AFTER ALL, THE FIRST TIME I SAW YOU—

OH, HOW ANNOYING.

Tsk.

LET ME THINK...

.....

THE FIRST TIME...?

WHAT... HAPPENED THE FIRST TIME?

!

SENSEI?

......

OH, SHUT UP ALREADY!

NO, IT'S MINE!

QUIET!

QUIET! QUIET! QUIET!!

......?

THIS IS...

...MY MEMORY, AND YET...

...WHY CAN I NOT REMEMBER OUR FIRST MEETING?

SE...

IT MUST HURT. YOU POOR THING...

WHY DO YOU ALWAYS FEEL SO MUCH PAIN?

DID THAT HURT?

BASH

WHAT?

THROB THROB

HE SOUNDS SOME-HOW...

I'VE NEVER UNDERSTOOD. YOU'RE SO RECKLESS.

YOW!!

WHY DON'T I HELP YOU?

...SCATTERED.

IF WE'VE BEEN FIGHTING FOR THIS LONG, THERE'S NO WAY YOU'LL TAKE ME.

OKAY, TAKI?

LET'S STOP THIS.

IT'LL BE A LOT EASIER ON YOU IF YOU JUST GIVE UP.

NO ONE WILL BLAME YOU FOR STOPPING HERE.

EVEN IF WE HATE EACH OTHER NOW, WE WERE ONCE FRIENDS.

AND BESIDES...

I DON'T...

...WANT TO KILL YOU.

THE TRUTH IS...

TAKI.

CAN'T YOU...

...COME WITH ME?

COME WITH ME.

HALF OF YOU IS LIKE ME, ALREADY. IT WOULDN'T BE SO WRONG.

YOUR FATHER WAS ONE OF US.

!

...SHE WAS OF A WORLD WHERE PEOPLE ABANDONED THEIR CHILDREN. WHY WOULD YOU WANT TO LIVE SOMEWHERE LIKE THAT?

YOUR MOTHER WAS MORTAL, BUT...

YOU COULD THINK OF THIS AS DIVINE RETRIBUTION.

SO... HOW ABOUT IT?

TAKE MY HAND.

!

HEH.

YOU HAVE THE SAME FACE. THE SAME EYES, AND THE SAME VOICE.

YOU REALLY AREN'T HIM.

AND EVEN SOME OF THE SAME MEMORIES, BUT...

AND ANYWAY...

...I NEVER MET MY PARENTS, SO I DON'T CARE WHAT "SIDE" THEY WERE ON.

...WHETHER IT'S A TRICK, OR IF THAT'S HOW YOU REALLY FEEL...

...IF YOU THINK I'M JUST GOING TO TAKE YOUR HAND AND SAY "YES"...

EVEN IF NONE OF US ARE RELATED BY BLOOD, I FOUND MY FAMILY HERE.

SENSEI WOULDN'T TELL ME TO GIVE UP.

...YOU'RE DEFINITELY NOT SENSEI.

I'M TURNING DOWN...

...YOUR OFFER.

SILLY CHILD.

SEN...

......
!!

BASH

WHA-!?

UH-OH...

THAT LIGHT...

I FEEL LIKE I'VE...

HUH...?

WHERE...

...WAS IT FROM...?

...SEEN IT BEFORE.

I'M ME.

SHIKIMI.

!

STILL

THUD

WHAT'S DIFFERENT ABOUT ME?

YOU SAY SUCH STRANGE THINGS.

I REMEMBER YOU. AND LAZ. AND AGI, TOO.

EVERYTHING THAT HAPPENED BEFORE YOU CAME.

I REMEMBER EVERYTHING THAT'S HAPPENED OVER THE LAST YEAR.

AND EVERYTHING THAT'S HAPPENED SINCE THEN...

I REMEMBER.

YES...I REMEMBER NOW.

THE FIRST TIME I MET YOU.

I REMEMBER WHY...

...I BROUGHT YOU BACK WITH ME.

WHY?

THAT'S RIGHT. THAT DAY...

I JUST HAD SOMETHING TO TELL HIS MOTHER.

RUSTLE

I HADN'T COME TO COLLECT THE DEBT.

I WANTED TO TELL HER...

...NOT TO WORRY ABOUT THE MONEY.

I HAPPENED UPON HIM BY CHANCE.

IT WAS PURE CHANCE THAT I MET THIS NIGHTLING.

BACK THEN...

...I WAS UTTERLY TERRIFIED.

FOR A MOMENT...

FOR ONE FLEETING MOMENT...

THAT'S WHY I TOOK HIM WITH ME.

I THOUGHT IF THEY WERE THAT FRIGHTENED...

IT ONLY LASTED A MOMENT, AND I WAS CAREFUL NOT TO REACT.

THE FEAR I FELT WAS THE DEMONS WITHIN ME.

...THEN MAYBE...

JUST MAYBE...

KICK

...THIS BOY...

...WOULD STAND A CHANCE AGAINST THEM.

I FELT THE SMALLEST BIT OF HOPE.

CLANG

NGH!!

SWIPE

CLANG

SLICE

BANG

GRIP

SLICE

SLICE

DUCK

SLASH

. . . . . .

REMARKABLE.

RETREAT

HE'S SIMPLY LOST HIS HESITATION. HE'S MORE DETERMINED.

IT'S NOT THAT HE'S MORE ACCURATE...

...OR MORE AGILE. HE'S NOT FASTER.

THAT'S ALL.

AND YET...

THAT'S ALL IT IS.

IT'S LIKE THE FIRST TIME WE MET.

AND YET, WHAT IS THIS FEELING?

...OF THIS BOY?

BECAUSE HE'S A NIGHTLING?

IS IT FEAR...

. . . .

HE'S FAST.

RUSH

TENSE

I HAVE TO SNUFF IT OUT.

IT'S TAKING EVERYTHING I'VE GOT TO NOT GET HIT.

THIS ISN'T GOOD...

| | | |

I HAVE TO EXTIN-GUISH...

...THAT LIGHT.

...HM?

FALL

STOMP

!

WAIT.

THAT LIGHT...

WHAT IS IT...?

THUD

CATCH

I CAN'T GET AWAY, BUT...

IT'S OVER.

BUT...

I WON'T BE ABLE TO DODGE THIS.

UH-OH.

DRIBBLE

...I KNOW SENSEI.

THUNK

I KNEW IT.

HE MISSED.

SO...

YOU HAVE TO LEECH OFF HUMANS TO SURVIVE, RIGHT?

RUSTLE

SINCE YOU DON'T HAVE YOUR OWN BRAIN, YOU HAVE TO USE THE BRAIN OF YOUR HOST.

I CAN'T HAVE MISSED AT SUCH CLOSE RANGE.

H...

HOW...?

WHY...!?

SO HOW...?

...SENSEI WOULD NEVER WANT TO HURT ANYONE.

EVEN IF IT'S JUST THEIR BASIC INSTINCTS AND BEHAVIORS AND MEMORIES...

AND THAT'S INFLUENCED BY THE HOST'S PERSONALITY.

YOU REALLY...

...HAVE SUCH HIGH STANDARDS FOR HIM, TAKI.

YOU'RE SAYING YOU KNOW ME BETTER THAN I KNOW MYSELF?

THAT IF I DON'T LIVE UP TO THE IDEAL IN YOUR HEAD, I'M NOT ME?

ACTUALLY, YOU'RE A FOOL.

WHAT BASIS DO YOU HAVE FOR BELIEVING THAT?

WAFT...

YOUR SMILE...

GIVE ME A BREAK.

AS YOU SAID BEFORE, THIS PERSONALITY...

...IS ME.

YOUR UNCONDITIONAL TRUST...

I SWEAR...

AND YOUR IRRESPONSIBLE OPTIMISM HAVE ALWAYS IRRITATED ME. YOU KNEW THAT.

I SHOULD HAVE NEVER FOUND YOU.

I SHOULD HAVE DONE THAT IN THE FIRST PLACE.

I'M DISAPPOINT-ED.

I HAD ALWAYS WANTED TO USE THESE HANDS...

I'VE HAD ENOUGH.

IF I CANNOT KILL YOU, I WILL SIMPLY ABSORB YOU.

....

WHEN WE FIRST MET...WHEN I FIRST SENSED YOU WERE A NIGHTLING...

...I SHOULD HAVE TORN OUT YOUR THROAT AND FEASTED ON YOUR BLOOD. IT WOULD HAVE SAVED ME A LOT OF TROUBLE.

...TO RIP YOUR HEART FROM YOUR CHEST!

I'LL KEEP YOU LOCKED UP IN DARK-NESS FOR ETERNITY.

THAT'S A RATHER VIOLENT THING TO SAY.

IT DOESN'T SOUND LIKE ME AT ALL.

...IS COMPLETELY TRUE.

ALTHOUGH, WHAT YOU SAID ABOUT HIS SMILE...

WAIT...

HOW?

SEN...

··········

THE REST IS JUST VENTING.

I'M SORRY. PLEASE DISREGARD IT.

YOU'RE A STUBBORN ONE.

I THOUGHT YOU'D HAVE VANISHED COMPLETELY, BY NOW.

IF YOU INSIST ON HANGING AROUND, I WILL INSIST YOU REMAIN SILENT.

YOU CAN'T.

YOU HAVE NO POWER OVER ME.

IF YOU INTEND TO GET IN MY WAY, I'LL GET RID OF YOU FOR GOOD.

...I WILL ACKNOWLEDGE...

...COME AGAIN?

...THAT YOU ARE ME.

THE PART OF ME I ALWAYS TRY TO DENY.

A COWARD ALWAYS BLUFFS, AND PEOPLE ALWAYS RESENT WHAT THEY CAN'T HAVE.

EVEN WITH THE DEMONS AND VIOLENCE AND EXTREMES...

YOU CAN'T GET RID OF ME.

BUT RIGHT NOW I'M THE ONE WHO'S A PART OF YOU.

I AM YOUR HOPE.

AND, LIKE MYSELF...

...YOU CANNOT BRING YOURSELF TO GIVE UP HOPE.

BECAUSE LIVING MEANS HAVING HOPE.

I WON'T DISAPPEAR.

I'LL KEEP COMING BACK AS LONG AS YOU NEED ME.

I WILL CONTINUE TO FEEL THESE EMOTIONS YOU SO DESPISE.

AND YOU KNOW YOU CANNOT HIDE...

...FROM THAT WHICH IS INSIDE YOU.

I'M NOT EXAGGERATING.

EVEN IF THE SMALLEST WISH, THE FAINTEST GLIMMER...

IT'S AN ESSENTIAL EMOTION...

...IF ONE IS TO LIVE.

...IF A HEART YEARNS FOR SOMETHING HARD ENOUGH, IT CAN BECOME A POWER TO BE RECKONED WITH.

IF YOU DESPISE LIFE THAT MUCH, LEAVE THIS PLACE.

THIS WORLD IS NOT FOR YOU.

YOU...

IF THIS ISN'T MY WORLD, THEN I'LL CHANGE IT TO BE SO!

THAT'S RIGHT.

YOU'RE KIDDING ME!

WHY SHOULD I BE THE ONE TO LEAVE!? WHY SHOULD I SURRENDER!?

...WHY NOT TAKE TIME TO ENJOY MYSELF?

I'VE PLENTY OF IT.

I'LL FILL THIS WORLD WITH HATRED.

WOULD YOU STILL TALK ABOUT HOPE THEN?

I THOUGHT IT BORING TO KILL HUMANS ONE BY ONE, BUT...

PERHAPS I SHOULD CONTINUE WHAT I STARTED.

THAT'S THE KIND OF WORLD...

...I BELONG IN.

I'LL DROWN THE LAND IN BLOOD, AND BLOCK THE SUN WITH DESPAIR!

YES. THAT IS MY WISH!

SLAP

WHAT ARE YOU?

STUPID?

IT DOESN'T SEEM LIKE YOU REALLY WANT TO.

IT DOESN'T MAKE ANY SENSE.

FROM WHAT I HEAR, YOU HATE THEM.

IF YOU REALLY HATE THEM THAT MUCH, YOU *COULD* HAVE KILLED EVERYONE BY NOW.

BUT YOU CAN'T STAY AWAY FROM US, EITHER.

WHY CAN'T YOU JUST...

YOU'VE HAD PLENTY OF CHANCES TO KILL *ME*.

SO WHY DO YOU KEEP COMING BACK?

...LEAVE HUMANS ALONE?

THAT WORLD...

THAT WORLD YOU WERE TALKING ABOUT ISN'T WHAT YOU WANT.

YOU NEED PEOPLE TO SURVIVE.

YOU SAID THIS WORLD IS NOT FOR ME.

THEN WHERE...

WHAT WORLD IS?

DO YOU EVEN UNDER-STAND?

...CAN I GO?

IN THIS CAGE OF FLESH. THESE SHACKLES OF THE MIND.

THERE IS NO SUCH PLACE.

I HAVE NOTHING IF I'M NOT LIVING OFF HUMANS.

THE ONE WHO'S TRAPPED HERE IS ME.

I'M OPEN TO SUGGES-TIONS.

WHAT ARE YOU SAYING I SHOULD DO?

OKAY?

IF THERE IS NOWHERE I CAN GO...

...I'LL JUST CARVE OUT A PATH IN THIS ONE.

I HAVE NO OTHER OPTIONS.

A WORLD I CAN LIVE IN...

YEAH...

I KNOW HOW HE FEELS.

...AND ME.

YOU'RE RIGHT.

YOU...

WE'RE THE SAME.

HIMboo

...HAVE NO...

...A LOST CHILD.

...REAL HOME, DO YOU?

THE OLD ME.

HE'S JUST LIKE...

WHILE YOU'VE BEEN JUMPING FROM HOST TO HOST, YOU'VE BEEN INFLUENCED BY EACH ONE.

SO YOU DON'T KNOW WHERE YOU SHOULD BE.

YOU DON'T KNOW WHERE YOU CAME FROM.

AND NOW YOU'VE TAKEN SENSEI'S BODY, AND HIS PERSONALITY WITH IT.

DON'T YOU SEE WHAT HAPPENED?

SO VERY CHILDLIKE.

HE'S STUBBORN AND DETERMINED, BUT...

...HE STILL LOOKS LIKE...

...A LOST CHILD ABOUT TO BURST INTO TEARS.

YOU'VE TAKEN...

...HIS LONELINESS, TOO.

COME, NOW.

THIS HAS GONE ON...

...LONG ENOUGH.

DON'T YOU THINK?

TAKI.

SEN...

!

THANK YOU FOR BELIEVING IN ME TO THE VERY END.

IT'S UP TO YOU NOW.

I'M SORRY.

IT'S TIME...

...TO FULFILL YOUR PROMISE.

COUGH

COUGH

RRRUSH

RRRIP

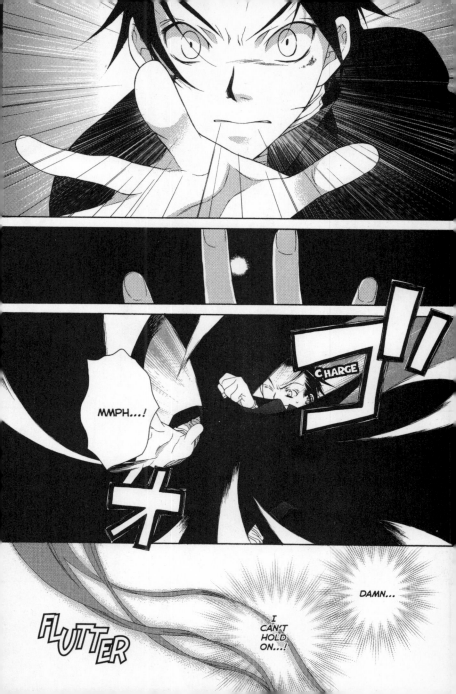

MMPH...!

CHARGE

DAMN...

I CAN'T HOLD ON...!

FLUTTER

THANK YOU.

YOU'RE WELCOME.

SO ALL THE SOULS...

...HAVE BEEN SET FREE. THAT'S GOOD.

BUT...

...THERE'S STILL THIS ONE.

COME! DEMON!

IF YOU HAVE TO LIVE OFF A HUMAN...

IF YOU MUST HAVE A HOST...

...THEN TAKE ME!!

I'LL GIVE YOU MY BODY, SO...

...LEAVE SENSEI.

AND COME TO ME!!

THADUMP

STAGGER

THADUMP

THADUMP

THADUMP

IT'S...
HERE.

...IS
INSIDE
ME NOW.

SOMETHING...

SWAY

FLAP

!

SE...

SEN—

WORDS CAN BE FREELY INTERPRETED.

I TOLD YOU...

...YOU SHOULDN'T BE SO QUICK TO DEAL.

YOU COULD DIE FROM INJURY OR ILLNESS, OR...

...WHEN IS THAT?

YOU KNOW...

YOU SAID "WHEN YOU DIE", BUT...

YOU COULD ALSO DIE BY SOMEONE'S HAND.

CHOMP

SUCK

SUCK

SUCK

SHLIP

PLIP PLIP

!

SHLIP

SUCK

SUCK

THUD

STEP

LUNGE

IT'S YOUR OWN FAULT.

....

WHY...?

I TOLD YOU TO FINISH ME OFF.

SO WHY?

I WAS SO CLOSE TO RECONSIDERING...

I THOUGHT MAYBE YOU WEREN'T JUST A MONSTER.

I THOUGHT... MAYBE I'D ALWAYS HAD THE WRONG IMPRESSION.

POOR TAKI...!

YOU DIDN'T HAVE TO TAKE HIM, TOO!

WHY DID YOU DO THAT!?

YOU DEMON...!

TO HEAL THESE WOUNDS QUICKLY, I NEED BLOOD.

SAVE YOUR BREATH.

IT WAS HIS END OF THE BARGAIN.

!

IT WAS A PERFECT DEAL.

LICK

I'D LEND HIM MY HELP, AND HE'D GIVE ME HIS BLOOD.

GRAB

WHY, YOU...!!

SETTLE DOWN, NOW.

THE BOY STILL LIVES.

DON'T PANIC. I DIDN'T KILL HIM.

WHAT...?

TAKE A GOOD LOOK.

...HE MIGHT BRING...

...A NICE LITTLE SURPRISE BACK.

BUT IF LEFT ALONE, HE'LL PROBABLY JUST DIE.

Taken care of like how!?

Should I give him CPR!?

ガバッ

GLOMP

Y... YOU'RE SURE!?

HE FAINTED FROM THE SUDDEN LOSS OF BLOOD.

AND IF YOU MANAGE TO RESUSCITATE HIM AFTER WHERE HE'S BEEN...

IF HE'S TAKEN CARE OF, HE'LL LIVE.

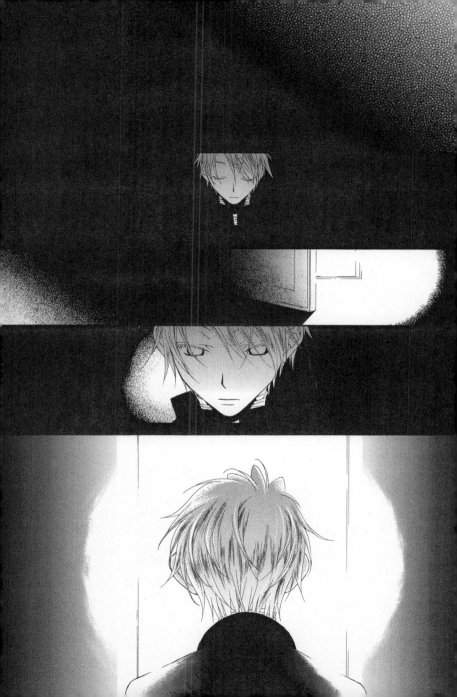

...HUH?

!

WHAT HAPPENED? WHAT WAS I DOING?

Wait, where are my glasses?

LET ME THINK...

TMP
TMP
TMP

BUMP

!

SENSEI!

WELCOME BACK!

IT'S GOOD TO BE BACK!

DID I MISS ANYTHING WHILE I WAS AWAY?

OH! THE LILIES IN THE GARDEN BLOS-SOMED!

AND THEN...

WAFT

．．．．．．

SHANI LEARNED HIS ABC'S!

OH, REALLY? THAT'S WONDER-FUL!

AH! HEY, QUIET!!

Ssh!!

AND ATTI BROKE A PLATE!

I'M HOME.

!

!

UUUH...

I FEEL LIKE I'VE DREAMED THIS BEFORE.

IT'S A DOOR.

AND IF I REMEMBER CORRECTLY, ON THE OTHER SIDE...

MAYBE I SHOULD OPEN IT?

WHERE HAVE I SEEN THIS BEFORE?

SOMEBODY TOLD ME ONCE, BUT...

...I CAN'T QUITE REMEMBER.

...THERE'S A BIRD...OR SOMETHING.

THE DOOR OPENS SO EASILY FROM HERE...

...BUT IT'S LOCKED TIGHT ON THE OTHER SIDE.

NOT THAT I'LL STOP YOU, IF YOU WANT TO GO.

IF YOU GO THROUGH IT, YOU CAN'T COME BACK.

YOU SHOULD STOP RIGHT THERE.

JUST A DEPARTED SPIRIT.

THERE'S A REASON I CAN'T GO THROUGH THERE YET, SO I'M WANDERING ABOUT ON THIS SIDE.

A mask?

W-WHO...

...ARE YOU?

IF YOU GO NOW, YOU CAN MAKE IT BACK IN TIME. THE FLESH SHOULD RETURN TO WHERE IT BELONGS.

I DON'T EVEN UNDERSTAND WHAT SHE'S SAYING.

THAT I SHOULDN'T GO, I GUESS.

NOW THAT I THINK ABOUT IT, BLONDIE WAS SAYING THE SAME THING.

BUT...

!

I FEEL LIKE I SHOULD OPEN IT.

BUT... WHAT'S THIS FEELING?

LIKE I HAVE TO OPEN IT.

HERE GOES!

RATTLE

THUD RATTLE

YOU'RE LATE, SENSEI.

WHAT WAS IT I WAS DOING...

...THAT TOOK ME SO LONG...?

YEAH? I...I GUESS I AM A LITTLE. SORRY.

YES, EVERYONE'S BEEN WAITING FOR YOU.

YEAH! WE WERE!

WELL...

That's right!

SENSEI?

WHAT'S THE MATTER?

!

UH...

HUH?

OH... NOTHING.

MY VISION'S A LITTLE FOGGY, IS ALL.

UH...I'M GOING SOME-WHERE...?

OF COURSE. IT'S STILL EARLY FOR YOU, SENSEI.

YOU'LL BE ABLE TO SEE BETTER ON THE OTHER SIDE.

AMARIA...

WHY DOES IT FEEL LIKE I DON'T BELONG?

AMARIA?

WHERE'S EVERYONE GOING?

WE ALL DECIDED...

SENSEI...

I'VE BEEN WAITING FOR YOU FOR SO LONG...

...THAT WE'D WAIT FOR YOU, SENSEI.

SO, JUST TELL US.

WILL YOU COME WITH US, OR GO BACK WITH THE BOY?

TAKI...

OH, YES... YOU CAN BRING HIM WITH US, IF YOU'D LIKE.

And why are you so little!?

TAKI!?

WH... WHAT'RE YOU DOING HERE!?

HOW ABOUT JUST SENDING HIM HOME?

CAN I DO THAT?

NO.

WE'RE GETTING FARTHER AND FARTHER AWAY FROM THAT DOOR...

EVEN AS WE SPEAK.

THAT DOOR IS TOO HEAVY TO OPEN FROM THIS SIDE ALONE.

BUT THAT'S—

LISTEN.

IF YOU GO, YOU PROBABLY...

BESIDES ...

...DO YOU REALLY THINK HE'D BE WILLING TO GO WITHOUT YOU, SENSEI?

YOU NEED TWO PEOPLE TO OPEN IT. YOU COULD JUST SHOVE HIM THROUGH, BUT...

...WON'T BE ABLE TO GET BACK.

THAT'S THE SPIRIT.

SENSEI ...

THERE'S NO CHANGING YOUR MIND.

YOU MUSTN'T LET YOUR-SELF GET LOST...

ALWAYS LOOK FORWARD.

SENSEI...

I'LL ALWAYS BE WATCHING OVER YOU.

THANK YOU FOR VISITING US.

BUT YOU HAVE TO GO, NOW.

DO YOU KNOW WHERE HEAVEN IS, SENSEI?

IT'S BEYOND THE FOREST... PAST THE EDGE OF THE WORLD.

PEOPLE...

YES... WE'LL BE VERY FAR AWAY FROM EACH OTHER, BUT...

...SPEND THEIR WHOLE LIVES STRUGGLING TO GET THERE.

SO YOU'RE...

YOU CAN REACH IT NO MATTER WHERE YOU ARE.

...YOU CAN'T GO TO HEAVEN, YET.

...GOING TO LEAVE ME ALONE, AGAIN?

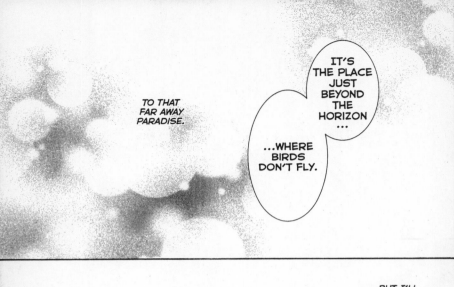

IT'S THE PLACE JUST BEYOND THE HORIZON...

...WHERE BIRDS DON'T FLY.

TO THAT FAR AWAY PARADISE.

BUT I'LL REACH IT EVENTUALLY.

AND I'LL GET TO SEE HER AGAIN.

NOW, THEN...

SHE SAID TWO OF US...

I GUESS IF WE BOTH OPEN IT, IT SHOULD WORK...

YOU SHOULD LEARN...

...A LITTLE MORE CAUTION, SENSEI.

...TAKI?

LET'S GIVE IT A PUSH...

...HUH?

RATTLE RATTLE

MURMUR YOU...

HUH?

SQUEEZE

THUD

WHA...?

キャラッ
KLATCH

...HUH?

!!?

SHOVE

SHUT

BLINK

LICK LICK
LICK

...WHAT JUST HAPPENED?

THAT SHOULD DO IT.

GOOD WORK.

Sure I can go through it, but...

YOU KNOW...

IT'S NOT NICE TO USE PEOPLE LIKE THAT.

THAT DOOR'S NOT OPENING FROM THIS SIDE.

IF HE'D STAYED HERE, YOU COULD BE WITH HIM.

BUT SENSEI COULDN'T HAVE GONE BACK ON HIS OWN.

Huh?

ALL THOSE LIES...WHAT IF HE'D SEEN RIGHT THROUGH YOU?

WOULDN'T THAT HAVE BEEN A GOOD THING? HE'S YOUR LOVER, RIGHT?

Isn't that how you are?

IT WAS NERVE-WRACKING, BELIEVE ME.

You know?

HOW ADMIRABLE.

DON'T BE SO RUDE.

I'M FINE WAITING.

WHAT!?

HOLD IT... YOU'RE STILL NOT DONE WITH ME!?

YOU PROMISED YOU'D HELP SENSEI LIVE THE LIFE HE CHOSE.

OH, IT'S NOT OVER YET.

FINE, WHATEVER. AT LEAST I'M FINALLY FREE.

I CAN'T BELIEVE HAVING YOU TAKE CARE OF *ONE* LETTER CAUSED ME SO MUCH TROUBLE.

YOU'RE JUST BEING OVERPROTECTIVE, NOW. SEE YA.

GIMME A BREAK ALREADY... HE DOESN'T NEED ME ANYMORE, RIGHT?

HE'S GOTTEN THIS FAR ON HIS OWN, HASN'T HE?

THANK YOU.

GRANDFATHER.

...

AWWW, MAN...

YOU'RE GRANDMA'S HUSBAND, AREN'T YOU?

YEAH, I GUESS I DID MENTION THAT...

I'D ALWAYS BEEN TOLD I GOT MY HAIR FROM MY GRAND-MOTHER, BUT I HEARD MY GRAND-FATHER WAS ALSO BLONDE.

AND YOU SAID YOU USED TO LIVE AROUND HERE, RIGHT?

And blondes are so rare around here.

WHEN DID YOU FIGURE THAT OUT?

Hm?

OH... SOMETIME ALONG THE WAY.

THANK YOU FOR SAVING ME.

AND...YOU LOOK A LITTLE LIKE MY FATHER.

...PLAY FAVORITES.

LOOK, DON'T GET THE WRONG IDEA. BEING RELATED HAD NOTHING TO DO WITH THIS.

IT WAS ALL BECAUSE OF THE DEAL, ALRIGHT?

Oh!

ALTHOUGH I WILL ADMIT, I DO TEND TO...

YOU SHOULD WAIT ON THE OTHER SIDE.

YOU CAN'T HANG AROUND HERE FOR LONG.

NOW, GO.

OH.

THAT'S RIGHT.

SHE SAYS SHE'S SORRY.

I ALMOST FORGOT.

IT'S HARD TO LOOK YOU IN THE FACE, SO IT MIGHT BE A WHILE UNTIL YOU SEE HER AGAIN.

I HAVE A MESSAGE.

WOULD YOU...

...GIVE HER MY REPLY?

FROM THE OTHER GIRL.

TELL HER, I'LL ALWAYS BE WAITING...

AND THEN...

...SO SHE SHOULD COME AS SOON AS SHE CAN.

...IT'LL BE JUST LIKE IT EVER WAS.

WHY DO YOU THINK WE WERE BROUGHT BACK?

YOU MEAN, WHY YOU WERE BROUGHT BACK AS A HUMAN?

I HAVE NO IDEA.

I'M STILL NOT SURE I REALLY WAS.

My body hurts so much I can't even move.

I DON'T MEAN THAT...

ZZZ

BUT...

BEING HUMAN SURE IS DIFFICULT, HUH?

I'M HUNGRY AND I HURT ALL OVER... AND IT'S ALL I CAN THINK ABOUT.

Ow, ow...

I'M STILL GLAD I'M ALIVE.

!

YEAH...?

!

ZZZ

I MEAN LATER. FURTHER DOWN THE ROAD.

NO, I DON'T MEAN THAT.

WHAT, INDEED. WELL, I DON'T THINK I'LL BE ABLE TO MOVE FOR A WHILE.

SENSEI.

WHAT'RE YOU GOING TO DO NOW?

YOU'RE TALKING ABOUT MY DREAMS FOR THE FUTURE? LIKE THAT?

I feel a little old for that.

YEAH. YOU WANNA OPEN A BAKERY OR A SHOE SHOP?

AND THEN...

I'LL LET MY BODY HEAL, AND GET MY STRENGTH BACK.

......

YOU MUST HAVE...

...SOME SORT OF IDEA.

WHAT DID YOU WANT TO DO BEFORE?

AH, YES.

BUT FIRST I WANT TO MAKE SOMETHING CLEAR.

THAT.

I DID HAVE AN IDEA.

STEN...

HUH...?

WHAT DO YOU MEAN YOU'RE GOING TO SEE THEM?

I HAVE TO LET THEM KNOW I'M QUITTING, AND HANDLE ALL THE PAPER-WORK...

OF COURSE, I MEAN *AFTER* I CAN MOVE, BUT...

...I THINK EXPLAINING EVERYTHING TO THE CENTRAL COMMITTEE IS THE RIGHT THING TO DO.

YOU IDIOT!!

YOU STAND OUT LIKE A SORE THUMB WITH YOUR HAIR LIKE THAT. YOU'LL BE PUTTING YOURSELF IN DANGER!

HAVE YOU FORGOT-TEN YOU'RE STILL A WANTED MAN!?

YOU DON'T HAVE TO GO! I'LL PROTECT YOU!

I TOLD YOU WHY I CAME HERE IN THE FIRST PLACE, RIGHT!?

I'VE ALREADY MADE UP MY MIND.

BUT...

I APPRECIATE YOUR CONCERN.

I AM NOT GOING MERELY TO RECEIVE PUNISHMENT. I PLAN TO CONVINCE THEM OF THE TRUTH.

IF YOU'RE GOING TO LIVE IN HUMAN SOCIETY, YOU HAVE TO FOLLOW THE RULES.

THERE'S ALWAYS A CHANCE THEY'LL HEAR ME OUT...

TAKI... WHAT'S THAT OVER YOUR SHOULDER?

HM?

I'M GOING TO HEAR THEIR VERDICT, AND PAY FOR MY CRIMES...

KNOCK KNOCK

YOU...

...SO I CAN BE PART OF THE WORLD AGAIN, AND LIVE WITH MY HEAD UP.

KLATCH

I'm coming in...

WHAT DO YOU MEAN, WHAT? I'M GOING HOME. MY JOB HERE IS DONE.

Uh...

WHAT THE...?

?

YOU STUPID OR SOMETHING!?

TAKI! SAY SOMETHING, WOULD YOU!?

HUH?

HUH? RIGHT NOW?

WHAAT!?

OH.

YEAH. EVERYTHING'S ALL SETTLED, AND IF I HURRY I CAN CATCH HI— I MEAN...

WELL, I'M GOING NOW, SHIKIMI.

UH, NOTHING...

UM... A-ARE YOU SURE YOU CAN'T STAY A LITTLE LONGER?

THERE ARE, AH... STILL SOME THINGS I COULD USE YOUR HELP WITH...?

WELL, ANYWAY. I'VE GOTTA HURRY, SO SEE YA!

AH...!

Y... YOU'RE RIGHT.

ARE YOU SURE?

I MEAN, YOU'RE FINE NOW, RIGHT?

IF YOU EVER NEED ME, JUST WRITE. I'LL COME BACK.

YEAH...

TAKE CARE.

AND THANK YOU.

TAKI, YOU IDIOT.

YOU BIG DUMMY-HEAD!!

!

IDIOT.

QUIET, YOU HEARTLESS JERK!!

WHAT ARE YOU, THREE?

Let go of me.

WAIL WAIL

WAIL

THAT'S WHY I'M LEAVING!!

I HAVE TO GO TAKE CARE OF THINGS BEFORE SENSEI CAN GET OUT OF BED!

BUT IF YOU LET HIM GO TO THE COMMITTEE, WHO KNOWS WHAT THEY MIGHT DO TO HIM!

WHY ARE YOU GOING HOME!? HOW CAN YOU LET SHIKIMI GO!?

I NEVER THOUGHT YOU'D DO SOMETHING LIKE THIS!

WHAT CAN I DO? YOU KNOW HOW STUBBORN HE CAN BE.

LOOK AFTER SENSEI FOR ME, LAZ.

AND DON'T FORGET TO EAT YOUR VEGETABLES! SEE YA!

And brush your teeth!!

ANYWAY...

...HUH?

LOOK, THAT'S ENOUGH! I'M IN A HURRY!

Got it?

SHOVE

JEEEEEERK!!

YOU JERK...

HUFF

HUFF

HUFF

YOU WERE GONNA LEAVE WITHOUT EVEN SAYING GOODBYE?

I FINALLY CAUGHT UP TO YOU.

YOU MUST HAVE KNOWN I WAS FOLLOWING YOU, 'CAUSE YOU DIDN'T SEEM TOO INTERESTED IN SLOWING DOWN.

YOU'RE LOOKING WELL.

HEART-LESS...

I THINK THAT'S A GOOD THING. SOUNDS LIKE YOU'RE HEALING NORMALLY.

IT'S PROOF THAT YOU HAVEN'T CHANGED.

Well, at least the skin healed.

I never said it wouldn't hurt anymore.

You liar. You said it'd heal in no time.

AND FOR YOUR INFORMATION, I'M NOT DOING WELL.

I HURT ALL OVER, AND MY SHOULDER IS BARELY HEALED.

And I'm still anemic!

WELL...

KIND OF LIKE WHEN YOU'VE EATEN TOO MUCH, OR EATEN SOMETHING BAD.

WELL, I DON'T THINK I'VE TRANS-FORMED OR ANYTHING, BUT...

...I DEFINITELY FEEL A LITTLE OFF.

ANY IDEA WHAT IT MIGHT BE?

...IT'S NOT REALLY BOTHERING ME.

THOUGH...

IT MUST BE THAT THING...

...THAT YOU MENTIONED.

THAT IMMUNITY I HAVE.

IT MUST BE REACTING TO THE DEMONS WITHIN YOU. WORKING AGAINST THEM.

IT'S YOUR BODY'S NATURAL DEFENSE.

IT ATTACKS ANYTHING IT DOESN'T RECOGNIZE.

BUT SINCE THEY'RE IN THE BODY OF A NIGHT-LING...

...AS LONG AS YOU'RE IMMUNE, THEY WON'T DIE UNTIL YOU DO.

WHEN THOSE LITTLE DEMONS LATCH ONTO A HUMAN, NOTHING CAN STOP THEM.

ANYWAY, WHY DON'T YOU COME BACK?

'Kay?

BLUNT

THANKS FOR ALL YOUR HELP.

I DIDN'T REALLY GET ALL THAT, BUT I THINK YOU SAID I'LL BE OKAY.

THAT'S RIGHT.

......

THAT'S ONE REASON YOU NIGHT-LINGS...

...ARE OUR NATURAL ENEMY.

STUPID DOG...

COME BACK ALREADY, IDIOT.

DON'T MAKE ME ASK AGAIN.

SHE'S TOO DUMB TO NEED MUCH ATTENTION.

I DON'T MIND LOSING A LITTLE BLOOD. IT'S NOT LIKE IT TAKES MUCH.

WELL, THEN...

WHAT CAN WE DO?

GLANCE

LOOKS LIKE YOU'VE BEEN FOUND OUT, AGI-CHAN.

COME NOW. YOU HEARD WHAT HE SAID.

HE'LL FEED YOU ALL YOU WANT.

IRK

I'LL BE FINE ON MY OWN. I ALWAYS AM.

AND YOU'RE A LIGHT EATER, SO YOU'LL BE FINE, TOO.

B...But...

BUT IF IT MAKES YOU FEEL BETTER... IF ANYTHING EVER GOES WRONG, I'LL COME GET YOU. OKAY?

Hmm...

...quit having conversations with the dog.

I know it's a little late to say this, but...

If big brother dies, Agi would be happy to die, too.

No, it's okay.

HM?

すりっ!!
RUB

CHOMP

CHOMP

BYE-BYE!

UNGH ...!!

CHOMP

!

WAIT!

FLING

!

I SAID YOU COULD HAVE MY BLOOD WHEN I DIED. I'M STILL ALIVE!

YOU JUST STOLE IT FROM ME, YOU SWINDLER!

HOLD IT!

COME ON, YOU! YOU BROKE YOUR PROMISE!!

'KAY?

CAN YOU JUST...

...DO ME ONE MORE LITTLE FAVOR?

LAZ.

MI...

SHIKI-MIIII!!

WHAT ARE YOU DOING UP!? JUST 'CAUSE YOU'RE FEELING BETTER DOESN'T MEAN YOU SHOULD PUSH YOURSELF!

BE RESPONSIBLE FOR ONCE, GO LIE DOWN!

YOU'RE NOT EVEN DRESSED RIGHT! IT'S A NICE DAY, BUT THERE'S STILL A BREEZE!

AND IT WAS SNOWING, REMEMBER!?

PULL

NO, NO, NO! IT'S BAD FOR YOU!

I'M FINE, I SWEAR. I NEED SOME EXERCISE.

I'VE BEEN IN BED FOR A MONTH NOW.

GET BACK INSIDE BEFORE I GET REALLY MAD!

I MEAN IT, I WON'T TELL YOU AGAIN!

BUT—

NO BUTS, MISTER!

YOU'RE RIGHT...

OKAY...

WHAT AM I SEARCHING FOR?

...NOT USED TO BEING WITHOUT HIM.

THIS ISN'T GOOD FOR ME.

I GUESS I'M JUST...

WHAT'S THE MATTER?

OH... NOTHING.

!

AND I SHOULD DO IT FAST.

I WANT TO SEND FOR HIM, ALREADY.

I NEVER REALLY REALIZED HOW LONELY I WAS, BUT...

AH!!

I THOUGHT I HEARD SOMETHING, THAT'S ALL.

...I SUPPOSE I'LL JUST HAVE TO GET USED TO IT.

HELLO, THERE!!

I SEE SOME-ONE!

SOMEBODY'S HERE!

Who is that?

CROWD

HUH?

What the...?

Now, now!

!!!

OH, HELLO THERE, SENSEI.

LOVELY WEATHER WE'RE HAVING, HM?

LOOK HERE, YOU RASCALS!

DON'T LEAVE YOUR MOTHER BEHIND LIKE THAT!

THANK YOU FOR TAKING SUCH GOOD CARE OF MY BOY.

I'M SORRY, THEY'RE JUST SO EXCITED...

Who are you!?

Wow!

What a big house!

Who are you!?

Wheel!

WHY? WHAT...

JUHAS-SAN?

HUH?

HUH?

WHAT'RE YOU ALL DOING?

...ARE YOU DOING HERE?

TAKI'S...

...MOTHER?

Your guys sure are clingy.

Play! Play with us!

I THOUGHT I SAID TOMORROW.

YOU GUYS ARE EARLY.

Oh! It's big brother!

Big brother!

Big brother!

WELL, I JUST COULDN'T WAIT...

YOU CAN'T JUST SHOW UP WHEN YOU FEEL LIKE IT, MOM. IT'S CALLED A SCHEDULE!

W...WAIT A MINUTE! TAKI!?

WHAT'RE YOU DOING HERE!?

Tee hee hee!

SCHOOL?

YEAH, WELL, WHAT ARE WE GONNA DO ABOUT ROOMS? THEY AREN'T READY YET!

OH, IT WON'T TAKE LONG IF WE ALL HELP.

UM, EXCUSE ME...?

THEY'VE NEVER GONE TO SCHOOL BEFORE...

OH, WHAT'S THE MATTER? EVERYONE WAS SO EXCITED, WE JUST COULDN'T WAIT TO LEAVE.

WA

Don't grow up too fast, you hear me?

Aaaw, a puppy.

Tee hee!

TAKI!! I'M TALKING TO YOU!!

P... PLEASE...

TELL ME WHAT THIS IS ALL ABOUT!

YOU DO NOTHING BUT READ BOOKS ALL DAY, SO YOU KNOW A LOT.

CHEW

WELL...

I WAS THINKING ABOUT WHAT YOU SAID, SENSEI.

WHAT DID YOU WANT TO DO BEFORE?

YOU SAID YOU WANTED TO TEACH SOMEBODY ABOUT EVERY-THING YOU'D LEARNED.

ABOUT WANTING TO BE A REAL TEACHER.

ONCE I GET BETTER, I PLAN TO GO TO THE COMMI—

OH, DON'T WORRY ABOUT THAT. I WENT ALREADY.

I mean, you've got more than enough rooms.

B... BUT...

IT WAS JUST HYPO-THETICAL, BUT...

As you can see, they're pretty enthusiastic.

SO I ASKED MY BROTHERS AND SISTERS IF THEY'D LIKE TO GO TO SCHOOL.

I TOLD THEM...

...THAT I'M A NIGHTLING.

Let's see, now...

RUMMAGE

...WHAT?

...I PROMISED TO WATCH OVER YOU, SO...

I LEFT OUT MOST OF THE DETAILS, BUT I GAVE THEM THE GIST...

...AND THOUGH THEY SAID THEY COULDN'T GIVE YOU A FULL PARDON...

...THE CENTRAL COMMITTEE WILL STAY OFF YOUR BACK FROM NOW ON.

See? They gave me this official document (even though I can't read it).

Oh wow, this is legit.

WELL, I BROUGHT GREY WITH ME, SO THEY WEREN'T HARD TO CONVINCE.

WHAT?

I DON'T EVEN KNOW IF I SHOULD ASK, BUT...

...DID THEY REALLY BELIEVE YOU? ABOUT BEING A NIGHTLING?

WHEEEE!!

THE MOMENT THEY SAW HIM, THEY WERE FINE. THEY WELCOMED ME RIGHT IN!

WE PRETENDED LIKE I'D CAUGHT HIM.

AFTER ALL, HE'S INFAMOUS AMONG DEMON VANQUISHERS.

WHAAAT?

DON'T EXAGGERATE. IT WAS JUST A LITTLE WHITE ONE!

AND GREY HAD FUN WITH IT, SO EVERYBODY WINS.

SO YOU *LIED.*

ANYWAY!

Well, it all worked out for the best, right?

You said he'd vanished when you left. It was all just a set-up, wasn't it?

I'm not going to say anything about this.

WITH THAT...

I LOOK FORWARD TO OUR PARTNER-SHIP!

And Agi, too.

...THE PLEASURE'S ALL MINE!

And Agi, too.

HEY, TAKI!

WHAT'RE YOU DOING? WHAT ABOUT EVERYONE'S ROOMS?

WHAT SHALL WE DO FOR DINNER?

Brother!

......

......

A Place Where The Birds Don't Fly + END

Bride & Mother-in-law

LOOK AT THIS DUST! YOU THINK THIS PASSES FOR CLEANING!?

IS THIS ANY WAY FOR THE WIFE IN THIS CHURCH TO BE!?

Dust

NOW, LOOK HERE! WHAT'S THE MEANING OF THIS, TAKIKO-SAN!?

OR ARE YOU DOING THIS TO ME ON PURPOSE!? WHAT KIND OF DAUGHTER-IN-LAW ARE YOU!?

WHAT KIND OF UPBRINGING DID YOU HAVE!?

I DON'T BELIEVE THIS!

IF YOU HAVE ANY COMPLAINTS, THEN YOU CAN JUST LEAVE!

I WON'T HEAR ANY EXCUSES. YOU CHEEKY LITTLE...!

QUIET!

BUT... MA'AM, I DIDN'T MEAN TO–

FINE, MOTHER.

I'LL GO HOME, THANK YOU VERY MUCH.

!

END

Theme provided by assistant Yosaki-san

Thorn & Splinter
いばらとげ

COME HERE!

ROSE!

ROSE, DEAR!

UMMM...

OH, I KNOW!

HM?

WHEN YOU GET OLDER, WHAT DO YOU WANT TO BE?

I WANT TO BE A WIFE FOR MY DADDY!

OR SO...

...SHE SAID.

SHE LIED TO ME...

NNN...

BROTHER...

SENS-EEEEI...

YAWN

THERE'S SOMEBODY HERE TO SEE YOU.

SILENCE

||||

Hm?

...ALWAYS THE WEIRDEST KINDS OF PEOPLE YOU CAN GET.

WHY DON'T YOU, SENSEI?

GET OUT EVERY ONCE IN A WHILE, WOULD YOU?

YOU HEARD HER. WE HAVE A GUEST.

BESIDES... THE KINDS OF GUESTS WE GET HERE ARE...

We're going back to naptime.

?

AREN'T YOU GOING TO GREET THEM?

I'M READING.

WHAT'S THE BIG DEAL? NOW, GO.

YEAH, WELL, I'M CLEANING!!

STOMP

NO, YOU GO.

STOMP

STOMP

STOMP

BAM

HOW LONG WERE YOU GOING TO MAKE ME WAIT FOR YOU, YOU ASSES!!

WELL, YOU—

NOW, LOOK HERE!!

I SWEAR, HOW BOORISH!!

WHERE'S ROSE!?

I CANNOT ALLOW MY DAUGHTER TO LIVE ON IN SUCH CONDITIONS. I'M TAKING HER BACK.

FREEZE

I...I'D HEARD IT'D GONE BACK TO NORMAL.

Great. Another weird guest...

DROOP

HAIR?

Mine?

ACTUALLY, HOLY WAIT A MINUTE!!

...AH, YES.

Welcome!

WH-WHAT'S WITH YOUR HAIR!?

WHERE'S ROSE!?

Ahem.

W...WELL, I'M NOT HERE FOR YOU, ANYWAY.

I ONLY CAME TO GET MY DAUGHTER BACK.

YOU MUST BE FROM THE CHURCH.

...my hair and eyes are still the same.

I'm back to human, but...

I THOUGHT I'D CUT OFF MY AFFILIATION WITH THEM.

OOOH...

DAUGHTER?

YOURS?

ROSE?

Huh?

IF YOU'RE LOOKING FOR HER, SHE'S OUT DOING THE LAUNDRY IN THE BACKYARD.

HUH?

WELL, YOU SEE...

BESIDES MY FAMILY, WE DON'T HAVE ANY GIRLS HERE.

UM...ARE YOU SURE YOU DON'T HAVE THE WRONG PLACE?

ARF?

IF YOU DARED TREAT HER WRONG, I DON'T KNOW WHAT I'LL DO TO YOU SCUMBAGS!!

ARF?

UGH!! WOULD YOU ALL PIPE DOWN!?

ARF?

ARF?

Huh? What's going on? Why's everyone yelling?

SHE'S DOING LAUNDRY!? YOU'RE MAKING MY DAUGHTER WORK AS A MAID FOR YOU, OR SOMETHING!?

WHOA, WHOA, WHOA. EXPLAIN WHAT'S GOING ON HERE, SENSEI.

F?

an Agi help? Agi's gonna yap her head off, too!

F?

WAIT, WHAT!? SENSEI, YOU'RE SAYING WE HAVE ANOTHER GUEST!?

...HUH?

YOU'RE ALL ADULTS, CAN'T YOU BE A LITTLE MORE...

...RE-SERVED?

WHAT'S ALL THE COMMO-TION?

DAD!?

ROSE!

!!?

YOU'LL WAKE THE CHILDREN UP, SO KEEP IT DOWN!

WHAT HAPPENED TO YOUR HAIR!? WHY'D YOU CUT IT!? HOW COULD YOU!!?

MY LITTLE ROSIE!!

Whoa.

HUG

Eep.

BASH

I'M SICK OF YOU, ALREADY!! GET A CLUE! I'VE FLOWN THE NEST, OKAY!?

WHAT ARE YOU DOING HERE, ANYWAY!?

TH...THAT HURT, ROSIE. WHAT'RE YOU—

SHUT UP, YOU IMBECILE !!

AND IN SUCH ROUGH LANGUAGE!

H...HOW CAN YOU SAY THAT TO YOUR OWN FATHER!?

THAT'S DISGUSTING!! NEVER HUG ME AGAIN, YOU PERV!!

NOW! COME HOME WITH DADDY!!

Uuuh...

STILL!! DADDY UNDER-STANDS YOU!

THAT'S WHAT HAPPENS WHEN YOU STAY IN A HOUSEHOLD FULL OF MEN. IT'S ALL THEIR FAULT! THOSE MONSTERS!

HUG

Yikes.

BASH

YOU'RE COMING WITH ME—

HUH?

DON'T...

I CAN'T LEAVE MY PRECIOUS DAUGHTER IN THE MIDST OF A GANG OF MEN!!

Y...YOU FOOL! BOYS AND GIRLS ARE DIFFERENT!

The only girls here are my mom and my little sisters.

SNAP

I WROTE YOU A LETTER! I'M NOT COMING BACK!

I'M A MAN!! YOU MORON!!

DON'T MAKE ME REPEAT MYSELF.

RRRRUMBLE

ALL MY BROTHERS GOT TO LEAVE HOME AT MY AGE! YOU NEVER GAVE THEM ANY GRIEF!

HOW...

SLAMO

Baldy!!

REMEMBER YOUR CHILDREN'S SEX, AT LEAST! YOU IDIOT!!

RO-

WHAT'S GOING ON HERE, SENSEI? WHY'S HE CALLING LAZ "ROSE"?

Sensei!! What do I do!?

FRET FRET

WAH!!

HOW CRUEL, ROSIE!!

UH... HUH? WHAT?

ARF!!

ARF!!

ARF!!

Agi's talking, too! Look at her talk!

I don't get this. I don't get any of this!

ARF!!

I'm not even going bald!!

Brother, I have to go potty...

What's going on?

Yaaawn...

I'm hungry.

ARF!!

ARF!!

Talking! Talking!

WHO'S THAT REFERRING TO?

LAZ... I MEAN, LAZLO WAS MY FATHER'S NAME.

A man's name!

I LOVED HIM VERY MUCH...

I SEE.

SO ROSE IS HER REAL NAME.

ROSE, IS IT?

YES, IT IS!

QUITE AN APPROPRIATE NAME FOR HER.

No, uh...

I MEANT HOW THORNY SHE IS.

You were asking for too much...

SHE'S AS LOVELY AS A ROSE!

I NAMED HER THAT, SO SHE WOULD GROW TO BE AS GRACEFUL, AND ADORABLE, WITH AS SWEET A SCENT AS A ROSE!

ARF!

W...WAIT! HOLD IT!

EXPLAIN ONE THING TO ME!

Should I keep talking?

ARF!

ARF!

CHOOOKE

WHAT DID YOU SAY!?!?

ALL THIS TALK ABOUT LAZ BEING "ROSE" AND YOUR DAUGHTER...

ARE YOU SAYING, HE'S ACTUALLY A SHE!?

WHAT ARE YOU GUYS TALKING ABOUT!?

Agi, too--

He seriously never noticed...

MMPH!

WHAT PART OF THAT BEAUTIFUL FLOWER OF A GIRL LOOKS LIKE A GUY TO YOU!?

Like I said, he asks for too much as a father...

WHA...!?

IS THERE SOMETHING WRONG WITH YOUR EYES!?

Mmph! Mmph! Agi, too! Mmph!

WHAT KIND OF UPBRINGING MAKES HER ACT THAT WAY!?

BUT HE KEEPS INSISTING HE'S A GUY!

H...HOW RUDE!!

AND ACTS GAY, EVEN!

......

Mmph! Mmph!

Mmph! Meana Mmph!

I JUST COULDN'T UNDO THE WORK I DID ON HER--

...WORK?

SHE'S MY LOVELY AND ADORABLE DAUGHTER!!

No more of your lies!!

SHE WAS BEING REARED TO BE AS GRACEFUL AS A BUTTERFLY, BEAUTIFUL AS A FLOWER!!

HMMM... SO THAT EXPLAINS IT...

I THOUGHT IT WAS ODD.

SHE SEEMED 100% CONVINCED OF HER SEX.

WELL, WELL, WELL...

YOU DID SOME WORK ON HER, HUH?

DROOP

Stop that.

PEOPLE CAN DO WORK ON OTHERS THROUGH SURGERY, PERSUASION, SPELLS, CURSES...

N...NO, YOU SEE, IT'S LIKE THIS—

HYPNOSIS, EVEN...

WHAT'S THIS ABOUT WORK?

CREW CREW

I SEE.

Sorry.

LICK

BUT...

SHE USED TO SAY SHE WANTED TO BE HER DADDY'S LITTLE WIFE!!!

BUT YOU GOTTA UNDER-STAND!!

WHEN SHE WAS LITTLE, SHE WAS SO AGREEABLE AND CUTE!!

NUZZLE

We friends now?

WAAAH!!

AND YET...

DADDY'S...

...LITTLE WIFE!

Haaaah...

THAT'S NOT GONNA HAPPEN.

THAT'S WHAT SHE'D SAY.

IF I'M GONNA MARRY, IT HAS TO BE SOMEONE OTHER THAN YOU, POP.

GROW UP, AND LET THAT GO.

SHOCK

DOOM

...RIGHT NOW I WANT TO BE LIKE MY FATHER AND BROTHERS, AND BECOME...

OF COURSE I DO. NOT LIKE I'M THINKING OF DOING IT ANY TIME SOON, BUT...

Sheeesh...This is why mom left you.

R... ROSIE!?

D-D-DO YOU MEAN THAT!?

DOOOO

GRAB

...A DEMON VANQUISH

DROP

WHAT'RE YOU—

!?

NOW, ROSIE, THINK IT OVER.

...HM?

Huh?

CLAP
ばん!

!

?

THINK ABOUT WHAT KIND OF MAN YOU'RE GOING TO MARRY IN THE FUTURE, OKAY?

I WON'T ALLOW THAT.

I WON'T LET YOU FALL IN LOVE WITH OTHER MEN.

Only your dad.

...OTHER MEN!!

YOU WON'T MARRY...

HUH?

WHAT'RE YOU TALKING ABOUT? I'M NOT MARRYING ANY MAN.

I'M A DUDE!

BASH

WRIGGLE

Whoa! Action!

EVEN SAYING SHE'S BECOMING A DEMON VANQUISHER...

I knew she'd succeed taking after her old man's prowess, but still...

NO MATTER HOW MANY TIMES I TRIED, I JUST COULDN'T CHANGE HER BACK.

SHE'S LIKE HER BROTHERS. WITH HER CRUDE LANGUAGE, AND VIOLENT WAYS...

SOB SOB

AND...

AND THEN...

SNIFFLE

WAH!

She went to apply while I was at work.

THEY... THEY SAID GIRLS CAN'T BECOME VANQUISHERS, BUT...

...SHE INSISTED SHE WAS A GUY, AND GOT HERSELF INDUCTED...

LET US TAKE A GOOD LOOK, FOR THIS IS A RARE OCCASION.

IS THAT SO? MINE, TOO.

SENSEI...

THIS IS MY FIRST SIGHTING OF A TRUE MORON.

!!!

WELL, DUH.

THOSE EYES ARE THE SAME MY SONS SHOWED ME WHEN I TOLD THEM THE STORY!!

THOSE EYES!

WAAA

What?

BUT...I CAN'T DO THAT, NOW.

It's too hard!

IF YOU MESS UP AND TREAT HER LIKE A GIRL, SHE'LL JUST SLUG YOU LIKE ALWAYS.

THINK OF IT AS HAVING ONE MORE LITTLE SISTER.

TAKI...

HM?

I feel so worn out.

Me, too.

WELL, SOMETHING MUST HAVE CONVINCED HER TO BE A GUY.

Don't marry a man →

Why not? →

Because you're a guy!

Little sister...

...I GET IT.

SQUIRM

WRIGGLE

YOU'RE DONE HERE. GO BACK TO YOUR WORK.

AND DON'T MENTION ANY OF THIS TO LAZ. JUST ACT NORMAL.

Though she did end up falling for a guy.

IT COULD BE SOMETHING RATHER SIMPLE.

BY THE WAY, YOU KNEW LAZ WAS A GIRL, DIDN'T YOU?

BECAUSE IT WAS MORE FUN THAT WAY.

WHY DIDN'T YOU TELL ME?

....

Grey probably knew, too.

HEH ☆

WHAT!? DON'T YOU DARE WORK HER LIKE A SERVA—

THANK YOU, TAKI.

BASH

SO EASY TO CONVINCE.

WELL, TIME TO TELL HER TO GET DINNER READY.

OKAY. THEN I'LL ACT JUST LIKE I ALWAYS HAVE.

.....

IN ANY CASE...

WHERE'S MY DAD? HE GO HOME, YET?

LAZ.

PERFECT TIMING. I WAS LOOK-ING FOR YOU.

IS IT REALLY OKAY TO LEAVE HER AS SHE IS?

NO... SENSEI'S TRYING TO CALM HIM DOWN.

N...NOW NOW, DON'T BE MAD.

SURE HE'S A LITTLE (A LOT) STRANGE, BUT HE'S A GOOD FATHER TO BE WORRYING ABOUT YOU.

He's still here!?

TSK!

HM?

BUT...ISN'T BEING A GIRL MORE CONVENIENT FOR YOU?

I DON'T NEED HIS WORRY.

HE TREATS ME DIFFERENTLY THAN MY BROTHERS.

WHAT?

YOU KNOW, LIKE... HOW YOU LIKE SENSEI.

AND WHO'S EVER HEARD OF A PARENT WHO'D MESS UP THEIR KID'S GENDER?

Even giving me a girl's name!

THUMP

HE'S NOT LIKE OTHER PEOPLE.

IF I WERE A GIRL, I DOUBT HIS ATTITUDE TOWARD ME WOULD CHANGE.

SENSEI'S A GUY, SO IF YOU'RE A GIRL, THEN...

IDIOT.

I'VE BEEN OFFICIALLY REJECTED, AND AM NOT GETTING ANY SYMPATHY.

IT PISSES ME OFF, BUT AT LEAST HE'S TREATING ME LIKE AN EQUAL.

It's important for a man to know when to quit.

THAT'S TRUE.

BESIDES, I'M THROUGH PURSUING THAT.

HOW LIKE A MAN.

RIGHT!? SO WHY'S MY DAD STILL GET IT WRONG!?

I JUST WANT TO BE A SOURCE OF STRENGTH TO HIM AS A GUY.

TUG

SO IF HE'S HAPPY HOW HE IS NOW, THAT'S ALL THAT MATTERS.

HE'S ALWAYS BEEN LIKE THAT. TREATING ME DIFFERENTLY FROM THE REST.

IT'S 'CAUSE I'M THE YOUNGEST KID. COMPARED TO MY BROTHERS, I'M ALWAYS THE BABY.

BUT SINCE WE'RE ALL HIS CHILDREN, I WANT TO BE TREATED EQUAL TO THEM.

YOU'LL ALWAYS BE TREATED DIFFERENTLY DEPENDING ON YOUR AGE.

AND PARENTS AREN'T PERFECT.

BUT THAT'S A LITTLE HARD TO DO.

LA...

...HM?

HUH?

I MEAN, I'M GLAD I'M A GUY.

What was I saying?

HOW IT FEELS NOT BEING SEEN AS EQUAL...

I HATE IT.

I WISH I WAS A GUY...

HMPH

Uh. I mean...that was just a hypothetical situation...

AND BEING A DIFFERENT GENDER, EVEN MORE SO—

!!
Oops!!

HMM-MMM...

I'M PRETTY STRONG.

I MEAN, IF I FOUGHT MY BROTHERS, I'D HAVE A 50% CHANCE OF WINNING.

I GUESS HE DOESN'T EXPECT AS MUCH FROM ME.

We're all Demon Vanquishers in my house.

JUST LIKE MY DAD AND BROTHERS.

THAT'S WHY I BECAME A DEMON VANQUISHER.

Even though I quit.

I JUST WANT HIM TO RECOGNIZE THAT.

PAT

DOESN'T HE HAVE ANYTHING TO SAY?

COME ON.

WHAT'S GOING ON WITH HIM...?

FSS!

WHAT!?

I CAN'T BELIEVE YOU!! THAT'S NOT EVEN FUNNY!!

HMM? OH, I WAS JUST THINKING HOW YOU CAN BE SURPRISINGLY CUTE.

WHAT'RE YOU DOING!?

WHAT!?

NOOGIE NOOGIE

It's a compliment from your big brother.

Stop that!

SLICE

OW!

THAT GUY–

SO YOU ACTUALLY LOOK UP TO YOUR FATHER, RIGHT?

I compliment you, too.

YEAH, YEAH. LOOK, I'VE BEEN WORRIED ABOUT THAT.

That ragged edge.

I HAVE TO SAND THAT DOWN LATER.

THAT'S 'CAUSE YOU HAD TO SAY ALL THAT WEIRD STUFF!

OOOOWW...

UGH, THAT WAS SO STUPID.

MMMM...

LET ME SEE IT.

YOU GOT A SPLINTER IN HERE?

HE'LL PROBABLY DO THE SAME THING.

HE'LL STOP CARING ABOUT ME SO MUCH.

BUT, I...

HE'S TALL... LIKE MY BROTHERS.

....

THEY SUDDENLY GREW UP... AND GOT GIRLFRIENDS, SO THEY COULDN'T HANG OUT WITH ME ANYMORE.

WHAT BIG HANDS.

Lucky...

I...

HM.

LOOKS LIKE YOU'RE OKAY.

IF YOU HAVE AGI LICK IT, IT'LL FEEL BETTER IN NO TIME.

THERE WAS NO SPLINTER.

!

HM?

I...

HUH?

IF YOU LET HER LICK YOU, THE HEALING REALLY SPEEDS UP.

OH, DIDN'T I TELL YOU?

YOU JERK!!

I DON'T CARE IF YOU DON'T WANT TO HANG OUT WITH ME!

?

IT'S...

ARF!
ARF!
ARF!
ARF!

I'm not bald, even!!

Shut up, you idiot! 'Baldy!!

ARF!

Why do you have to be like that!?

Now do I get to join in?

Where do you get off suddenly calling me that!?

WHAT?

ARF!

Again?

I'D ALWAYS DREAMED OF DRESSING HER IN FLOWERS AND LACE, BUT...

WEEP WEEP

IT'S NO USE...

DROOP

SHE'S NOT COMING BACK. SHE'LL ALWAYS BE LIKE THAT.

SOB SOB

MY LITTLE ROSIE!!

I don't think girls usually walk around wearing flowers...

IT MIGHT ALREADY BE UNRAVELING.

IT'LL BE OKAY. AMATEUR HYPNOSIS LIKE THAT DOESN'T LAST FOREVER.

WHAT DO I DO!? WHAT MORE DO I HAVE TO LIVE FOR!?

LOOK, UH...

WAAAAH....

R... REALLY!?

WHEN!? HOW!?!?

MAYBE SHE'S ONLY CONVINCING HERSELF THAT SHE'S A GUY.

YOU DON'T HAVE TO WORRY. IT'LL FADE WITH TIME.

HMMM...

GOOD QUESTION.

IF THERE'S SOME KIND OF TRIGGER...

FOR EXAMPLE, WHAT HAPPENS IN FAIRYTALES SOMETIMES...

WHEN THE CHARACTER FALLS IN LOVE, OR SOME-THING...

DO SOMETHING ABOUT IT!!

WAAAAH!!

NO! I DON'T WANT THAT TO BE THE WAY SHE GOES BACK TO NORMAL!!

GYAAH!!

Ow! What're you doing!?

CHOMP

FUFF

JEALOUSY RISING

Thorn & Splinter + END

Number One

I'M TELLING YOU.

SO DON'T WORRY ABOUT IT, AND JUST LEAVE ME ALONE, TAKI.

I'M AIRING THEM ALL OUT. I'LL PUT THEM AWAY WHEN I'M DONE.

COME ON, SENSEI...

SHRUG

WELL, I REALLY FEEL LIKE CLEANING UP, THIS TIME.

I'D BELIEVE IT IF YOU NORMALLY BEHAVED THAT WAY.

BUT HOW IS THIS ANY DIFFERENT FROM THE USUAL SCATTERED MESS?

Who'll help me with this ribbon?

YEAH, YEAH. SORRYYYYY.

Ummm... Uuuh...

YOU KNOW THAT PISSES ME OFF!!!

THIS IS ALWAYS HOW IT GOES! YOU SAY YOU'RE GOING TO CLEAN UP, BUT THEN YOU FIND AN OLD BOOK, AND GET DISTRACTED READING IT!

IF THE RESULT'S JUST GOING TO BE THE SAME, THIS ISN'T ANY DIFFERENT!

CRASH

. . . . .

ド！！

UH-OH...

Well, well...

LOOK, I'M JUST SAYING YOU—

I'M REALLY NOT UP FOR ORGANIZING ALL THIS.

THIS IS IT. I'M GOING TO TEACH YOU HOW TO PUT THINGS AWAY. YOU'RE GONNA HELP!

You too, Laz!!

FINE, I GET IT.

!

HUH?

What a pain.

Alleyoop!

SCOOT

I gotta get over there.

Mmph!

SWAY

PLAY BY YOURSELF FOR A WHILE!

TOSS

...IT MIGHT BE DANGEROUS FOR LITTLE ONES. NO COMING IN.

You'll get all dirty, or hurt.

SORRY, BUT I'M GOING TO DO A THOROUGH JOB CLEANING TODAY, SO...

KLATCH

. . . . .

Huh?

Okay, let's do this!

SLAM

Uuuugh...

Brother

Hm?

But he's not here today...

I wanted them to tie this ribbon around me...

しょぼ〜ん...

DROOOOP

I...I think I got it wrong. Maybe it's backwards.

I'll wind it around the other way...

There, now you're adorable.

Yay!

I think he just wound it around me.

I know.

I got kicked out too...

とぼとぼ

PLOD PLOD

WRAP

...Huh?

STUCK

Just a little knot, and then...

DRAG DRAG

ROLL

It's all twisted...

STEP

RUSTLE
RUSTLE
SNAP
CRACK
ROLL
ROLL
ROLL
ROLL

?

?? ?

SIT

Hey-
Why are you
calling me
sister?

Sister? Sensei?

WANDER Brother... WANDER Home...

LOOK RUSTLE

LOOK DIG DIG RUSTLE

SIT

SOB

SOB

SOB

SOB
SOB

DRIBBLE

RUSTLE

JUMP

!?

Ha ha!

Heh heh!

RUSTLE

Gimme a kiss!

Good dog.

Awww, youuuuu...

NOT REALITY

TRMBL

TRMBL

TRMBL

RUSTLE

RUSTLE

RUSTLE

RUSTLE

RUSTLE

AWWW, THERE YOU ARE!

WHAT'RE YOU DOING OUT HERE, YOU IDIOT?

AWWW, YOU'RE COVERED IN DIRT.

I JUST GAVE YOU A BATH YESTERDAY.

THAT'S A NIGHTLING FOR YOU.

WHOA, YOU ACTUALLY FOUND HER, TAKI.

...HUH?

Here it comes...

IDIOT.

Hmph!

YEAH, WELL I'M THE ONE WHO SAID YOU HAD TO.

HEY, DON'T GO STEALING CREDIT.

As promised...

I washed her yesterday.

ACTUALLY, SHE'S STILL GOT A GRIP ON HIM.

HMMM?

AT LEAST SHE'S CALMED DOWN.

She fell asleep.

OW, OW, OW, OW, OW!

WHY THE LITTLE...SHE HAD HERSELF A CHEW FEST ON ME!

NO CRIES FOR HELP OR ANY-THING.

OH, NOTHING. I WAS JUST MARVELING HOW YOU'RE NOT TELLING ME TO TAKE HER FROM YOU FOR ONCE.

HM?

SMILE SMILE

SMILE

WHAT IS IT?

You're weirding me out.

I'M GLAD TO SEE YOU'RE MAKING UP FOR HAVING KICKED HER OUT.

YEAH, WELL WHOSE FAULT WAS THAT IN THE FIRST PLACE, HUH!?

SH...SHUT UP, YOU GUYS! I JUST CAN'T PEEL HER OFF, SEE!?

Look!

DANGLE

WE REALLY ARE NO MATCH FOR YOU.

NO MATTER HOW KIND WE ARE TO HER, WHO IS SHE MOST ATTACHED TO, HM?

DROOL

HMPH!

Indeed.

He's so stubborn...

Number One + END

Afterword

It's over.

This really is the end.

Thank you for sticking around for the whole long journey.

I'm fried.

WELL DONE.

Let me think... ABOUT FIVE YEARS, I GUESS.

It was a serialization that felt both long, and short.

I'm lying. It's been six and a half years. I still don't get why I answered that question so confidently with five, though.

REALLY, THAT LONG?

HOW MANY YEARS HAS IT BEEN?

This series has continued despite all the confusion, ups and downs, and struggles.

But now that I think about it, this has been my first serialization, and longest serialization.

It is a big relief to me that it ended safely.

But this is the second series I've come up with.

And my drawing style's changed a lot.

But while wrapping up the story, there was so much to do that I didn't really feel that "It's over!!" kind of feeling.

I suppose I'll feel it more strongly when the book is actually out.

Even to this day. Probably because I'm not done tweaking it here and there, still.

And, as always, when I had trouble figuring out what to write about here, my friend suggested...

So she gave me some material to use that's not really typical of my afterwords.

YOU SHOULD DO WHAT THE VOICE ACTORS ALWAYS DO WHEN THE ANIME'S OVER!

Thanks, friend...I think?

Oh, like what you're always doing...

WAAAAH!!

THE POOR THING'S GONNA END UP RUNNING AN ORPHANAGE (WATCHING OVER HIS SIBLINGS), AND ACTING AS A BODYGUARD (WATCHING OVER SHIKIMI)! IT'S JUST SO UNFAIR!!!

POOR THING!!

She's also very worried about Taki's future, for some reason.

POOR TAKI-KUN!

Thanks...?

Don't forget about dog-watcher, too.

Do something about it!!

?

There are a lot of people I have to apologize to, for all the trouble and pain I put them through.

My editors and those involved in the making of this book.

To my assistants:
Esaki-san, Yoko-san, Ling-san
And to everybody who read this!

Thank you so much!

Tomo Maeda

This is the final volume and my last chance to prattle on with all sorts of excuses, so I'm filling up these bonus pages with tons of tiny text. It hurts my eyes to read...

A PLACE WHERE THE BIRDS DON'T FLY

There were people who told me they worried for the characters' safety, but I like endings like this, which is why I ended it as you saw.

Not all the problems come to a perfect, solid ending, and our heroes might find themselves in lots of troublesome and difficult situations hereafter, but I think everybody ended up happy. So that's good enough, I think.

It lasted pretty long, but the story went in the direction I'd planned for. Please pay no heed to things that were not completely wrapped up, and plot points that looked like they'd go somewhere and then dropped out halfway along...After all, real life is filled with such mysterious phenomena, as well. Sorry...I know that's bad of me. The rest of this page is just my ramblings, excuses, things that came to mind, and other such drivel.

Having Shikimi's hair and eyes stay silver was based merely on a whim of mine. It makes for a nice visual balance on the page, I figured. Just think of it as taking its time to return to black.

As for injecting somebody with holy water to protect them from evil, I don't know if that's valid in Christianity or not. It doesn't really matter, I guess, since the Church in this story is for some kind of made-up Christianity. The main characters' clothes are also just symbols. Wondering why that's all they wear is just a waste of time. To you, my characters, I apologize.

Grey was adopted into his wife's family when he came from the West. So his children were left in their care, and kept safe after he died. I apologize for making this character so convenient and always taking advantage of him to do everything. I originally had his relationship with Amaria be a far more distant blood-tie, but it'd have made the name she calls him in the end sound so lame. "Grandfather of my great-grandmother!" is what it'd have ended up sounding like. And so I changed it. Also, I hadn't really planned on having his wife make an appearance, so I now deeply regret having gone with that pain-in-the-butt tone I used for her hair. I should've at least given her shorter hair to work with.

Just for fun, I decided to look up the last names of our characters, and they ended up being so appropriate for them, it made me laugh. Juhas means "shepherd" and Farkash means "wolf". Taki's so appropriately a shepherd, it's funny. But for Shikimi to be a wolf... In different countries, the wolf can be an animal that gets mistaken for a vampire. So for me to pick this most fitting of last names from the list I was referring to, is just bizarre. I swear, it was supposed to be a random drawing. Vargas meant "leatherworker" so it was a pretty normal name. By the way, these are all Hungarian names. And that "certain country" I wrote about in volume 6 was also Hungary. It's a country I'd like to visit, someday.

THORN & SPLINTER

The title was just whatever...Cuz the name Rose is similar to Laz. Also, cuz she's got a prickly personality.

Laz was originally made to offer the one bit of femininity to this manga full of ungraceful guys...but there wasn't really a reason why she had to appear otherwise. (Sorry.)

I'd originally planned for it to be that Laz was hypnotized by a guy who loved her but who she didn't like back, and he didn't want her to fall for any other guys. But right before sitting down to write that up, I was struck with the idea that if it was her overprotective dad instead, it'd be funnier.

I just don't get people who can keep professing their love to someone who doesn't even care for them in the same way. It's funny how in shojo manga, agonizing over unrequited love like that's supposed to be considered romantic. I think what Laz feels toward Shikimi isn't so much the romantic kind of love as adoration.

Since she's been rejected as clear as day, couldn't she find someone else to love? That's the kind of thoughts that surround Laz's behavior. So, this is how her story ends, but I think it'd be funny if she got dumped by Taki, too (she's practically already head-over-heels for him). Or maybe if she suddenly got really attached to Grey. I think it works out best to have her not revert to her original girl-side, but just stay the way she is. She makes for a good combo with anybody that way.

LAJOS VARGA

Bio:
45 years old.
I gave him a name,
but never even had
to use it...
And after
I'd worried so much.

Bio:
His sons
(Laz's brothers)
were only made
for this page here,
so they have
no names.

NUMBER ONE

I just love drawing little balls of fur. AKA, Agi. Though in the panels where she's really tiny, it can be a pain. That poor little pup just can't help getting herself into the least convenient situations. And even if somebody tried to explain things to her to help her out, I'm sure it'd go in one ear and out the other. The poor thing...

I really liked that make-believe memory she had of Taki saying "Gimme a kiss!"

ABOUT THE COLORS

I used color inks to paint the front cover, which feels like it's been a long time since last doing. I'm so happy the ink didn't smell this time.

For the sake of time, I'd moved away from this hands-on style for a year, so it's nice going back to it. The only trying part about it is that you can't make mistakes. So I've really gotta keep practicing. I want to get better.

I also came to the painful realization that I need to study color schemes, better. The color of the flowers are nothing like how I'd imagined they'd turn out.

Also, I have to be more conscientious of the printing part of the process. I had all these red flowers on the cover, but I wasn't firm enough with the hue and now they look too pink to me.

But anyway, thank you to everybody for reading up to the very end. I hope we can meet up again in whatever next work I do.

Well, goodbye.

Tomo Maeda

BLACK SUN SILVER MOON
Doujinshi Contest

In 2007, Go! Gomi and theOtaku.com teamed up with the first-ever New York Anime Festival to present a national *doujinshi* contest.

The entries were voted on by those attending the convention.

On behalf of the New York Anime Festival and theOtaku.com, we are proud to present the winning *doujinshi*:

"Hunting the Undead"
by
Lindsey Henninger

ELVESATEMYRAMEN

Hunting the Undead

ElvesAce@yRamen